Ramiz Daniz

Sensational map found in Istanbul

Science-popular essays

Baku -2022

Scientific editor and preface: - Academician Ramiz Mammadov
Editor: - Doctor of Philosophy in Technical Nadir Achmedov
Reviewer: Doctor of Philosophy in Geography Shamil Azizov
Translator: Hokume Hebibova
Computer design and computer operator: Sevinj Akchurina
Ramiz Daniz. "Sensational map found in Istanbul". 105 p.

Admiral Piri Reis made an atlas in 1528 and included this map in that atlas by fixing the date as 1513. Afterwards it turned out that, mentioned historical material was copied from ancient manuscripts kept in the library of Constantinople.

According to historical sources, Piri Reis often visited that library in order to analyze ancient documents and maps. Mentioned map could attract attention of Turkish scientists for its exactness. It was almost the first map, which described outlines of America. Besides it, the sensational material included outlines of North America and Antarctica. It was made 21 years after the first travel of Columbus. But the Genoese admiral hadn't visited the continent besides eastern coasts of Panama, Nicaragua and Honduras. Antarctica was discovered after more than 300 years by Fadday Bellingshausen and Mikhail Lazarev (1820).

Mackintosh's position is understandable, but it is not clear that he compares a map drawn in 1513 with maps of 1570 and 1599. That is, the Ribeiro map was produced in 15-25 years, the Ortelius map in 57 years, and the Wright Molinje map in 86 years after the Turkish admiral's map. It must be admitted that after 1515, most cities in Europe, where cartography was rapidly developing, began to produce maps with contours of the Caribbean, eastern Brazil, and North America.

The writer, researcher and publicist Ramiz Daniz was born in Baku in 1965. He graduated from secondary school in 1983. He has been a President grant holder since 2009 and he is a laureate of the *"Golden pen"* (2005) award. He is member of The Union of Azerbaijan Writers (1999) and Geography Society (2013).

He was winner of the international award instituted by the International Writers Union on 3 nominations in 2020 and Grand-Prix winner of the international award in 2021.

Preface - Sensational map found in Istanbul

The President's grant holder and laureate of the "Golden pen" award Ramiz Daniz (Gasimov) writes various literary and scientific works. His scientific works astonishes scientists of geography, astronomy and history of mathematics.

Ramiz Deniz has been studying geographical discoveries and their history for 38 years, and writing fictional and scientific works at the same time. His works have been entered in the libraries in Paris, London, New York, Prague, Madrid, Moscow, Beijing, Tokyo, Madrid and many other cities. Total 357 books including translations have been published in Russian, English, German, Spanish, Italian, French, Portuguese, Polish and Dutch by **"AV Akademikerverlag"**, **"Verlag Unser Wissen"**, **"JustFiction Edition"**, **"Lap Lambert publishing"**, **"Scholars' Press"**, **"Sciencia Scripts"**, **"Palmarium Academic Publishing"**, **"Our Knowledge Publishing"**, **"Novas Edições Acadêmicas"**, **«Edições Nosso Conhecimento»**, **"Editions Notre Savoir"**, **"Editions universitaires europeennes"**, **"Edizioni Accademiche Italiane"**, **"Sciencia Scripts"**, **"Edizioni**

Sapienza", "Wydawnictwo Nasza Wiedza", "Editorial Akademica Espanola", "Wydawnictwo Bezkresy Wiedzy", "Ediciones Nuestro Conocimiento", "Qlobe Edit" publishing houses of Europe. Most of them are distributed by 14 large advertising companies in more than 50 foreign countries. Most works of the author **"International science centre Maragino observatory", "Enigmatic discovery of Brazil", "Pope Alexander VI's demarcating line", "Letters, Paolo Toscanelli maps and Columbus calculations", "King Manuel's plan and discovery of Brazil", "Rich financers, who defended Columbus's project", "In XIII century, a famous scientist from Cordoba to Beijing", "Letters of Amerigo Vespucci compilation", "Transatlantic project of Columbus", "Brazil was opened in 1494", "The largest Academy of Sciences in the Middle Ages", "Columbus was aware of existence of America beforehand", "500 years of America's discovery", "Pedro Cabral and Amerigo Vespucci`s travelling to the Brazilian coast", "The scientist passed ahead of centuries – Nasiraddin Tusi", "Amerigo Vespucci, Martin Waldsemuller – secret bargain", "Learning the secrets of Cosmos in ancient times", "Nasiraddin Tusi and development of astronomy", "Christopher**

Columbus, Nasiraddin Tusi and discovery of America", "Fernand Magellan's expedition and conquerors of three oceans", attracted attention of the specialists.

Azerbaijan founds economical, cultural and political relations with other countries, integrates with the world and foreign countries are interested in science, education and culture of our country. That's why scientific research works of Ramiz Daniz may be interesting for scientists and ordinary readers, who learn the history of geographical discoveries. Probably he'll be invited to scientific conferences held abroad. Because Ramiz Daniz has found out many novelties and could deny most stereotypes.

He has described obscurities of Columbus's first travel and very interesting facts concerning the unknown map used by him during the expedition in his work **"Christopher Columus, Nasiraddin Tusi and real discovery of America".** R. Daniz has denied known information and mentioned that, Columbus knew the destina-tion, route and term of his travel, but kept it secret. Of course, this is a serious judgement. Reasons why three expeditions sent by Portuguese to the western part of the Atlantic Ocean in order to find the forth continent failed have been explained in the work. The author has proved by indicating perspicacity of Spanish monarchs and disbelief of the king of Portugal that *"Mathematical Union"* of Lisbon had significant role in appropriation of those territories by Spaniards. Besides it, Ramiz Daniz has mentioned that, Columbus had used calculations of scientists of the East including Nasiraddin Tusi when he prepared his project.

"Enigmatic discovery of Brazil" concerns the problem, which make scientists of geographical discoveries to hesitate, and the author tries to prove that Brazil wasn't discovered by Pedro Cabral in 1500 by accident, it was discovered by Duarte Pereira in 1494 in accordance with secret agreement reached with the king of Portugal, but the result of that travel was kept secret for some reasons. In accordance with this work, Portuguese were able to conceal Spaniards by means of the Pope and became owners of today's Brazil according to Tordesillas treaty concluded in 1494. Though Portuguese were agree to own lands located at 100 liq west of Azores in 1493, in accordance with the result of the secret expedition of Duarte Pacheco, who visited American coasts after a year, they appropriated large territories by moving the demarcation line between Spain and Portugal for 270 liq towards the west.

The author has described scientific activities and achievements of the remarkable scientist N. Tusi, essence of most of his works known all over the world in his next work *"The scientist passed ahead of centuries – Nasiraddin Tusi"* and mentioned that, several works of the scientist had been published by other authors as their own works.

It is known that, Nasiraddin Tusi wrote masterpieces in fields of astronomy, mathematics, geometry and ethics, played a significant role in development of these sciences and passed ahead of well-known scientists for hundreds of years. The author has remembered scientific works carried out by the most ancient scientists of Greece, ancient Rome, Byzantine, Egypt and Muslim scientists of the early middle ages, mentioned that, Nasiraddin Tusi had significant achievements in listed branches and tried to emphasize Tusi's genius.

According to the book, the astronomical table *"Zij-i Ilkhani"* prepared by Nasiraddin Tusi was used for discovery of America. Ramiz Daniz mentioned it in the book, which explains most issues concerning Tusi's scientific activity and causing scientists of the world to think. The scientist had described the prime meridian at 34^0 west of today's Greenwich Meridian (remote north-western coast of Brazil) and this fact helped Columbus when he passed the ocean.

Another interesting moment is the investigation of the real owner of the map made by the Turkish admiral Piri Reis in 1513, which has been analyzed in most science centers.

The author says that, part of that map, which was made of ancient manuscripts, was made in Maragha observatory under the leadership of Tusi. Besides it, he has mentioned that, Columbus had sailed to coasts of the New World by means of that map. According to R. Deniz, Piri Reis could find it afterwards together with the scientist's notes.

Most scientists had used Tusi's *"Zij-i Ilkhani"* when they made their astronomical catalogues. The Russian scientist Lobachevski and other scientists of geometry had made use of *"Tahriru Uglidis"* and German scientist Regiomontanus published a copy of *"Shaklul-qita"* as his work. Isaac Newton's teacher John Vallis read lectures at the University of Oxford in accordance with *"Tahriru Uglidis"* and played a significant role in popularization of Nasiraddin Tusi in England. Besides it, Copernicus had used Tusi's theorem "Two circles, one's diameter being equal to half of another one's, are on the same plane", which he had proved in his work *"Memories about astronomy"*, in his work *"About rotations of celestial spheres"*.

Piri Reis made an atlas in 1528 and included this map in that atlas by fixing the date as 1513. Afterwards it turned out that, mentioned historical material was copied from ancient manuscripts kept in the library of Constantinople.

According to historical sources, Piri Reis often visited that library in order to analyze ancient documents and maps. Mentioned map could attract attention of Turkish scientists for its exactness. It was almost the first map, which described outlines of America. Besides it, the sensational material included outlines of North America and Antarctica. It was made 21 years after the first travel of Columbus. But the Genoese admiral hadn't visited the continent besides eastern coasts of Panama, Nicaragua and Honduras. Antarctica was discovered after more than 300 years by Fadday Bellingshausen and Mikhail Lazarev (1820). That's why most scientists made radical steps in order to analyze the map. Author of the map and date of its preparation were interesting for them.

The American secretary of state Henry Stimson also was interested in this investigation. He thought that,

"Columbus's map" could be in Turkey. He ordered the ambassador of USA in Turkey to start researches in order to find mentioned map. Though the Turkish government supported researches comprehensively, any success couldn't be achieved.

Piri Reis mentioned that, he had used about twenty maps made during the age of Macedonian Isgandar in accordance with exact calculations. But scientists didn't believe his explanation about the map found in 1929.

Scientists couldn't believe the Turkish admiral's statements as aerocosmic technology didn't exist then. There wasn't any copy of maps made during the age of Macedonian Isgandar. The Turkish admiral's map caused great resonance in Turkey.

The map was published in many editions in the state publishing house in 1935 in accordance with the order of the president of Turkey Mustafa Kamala Ataturk, who was proud that, cartography had been developed in Turkey even in XVI century.

Ch. Hapgood came to the following conclusion when analyzed the map: "Exact information is exchanged between nations. The map was made by unknown nation and was found by Phoenicians and Creteans, who were considered genius seamen during more than thousand years, in ancient times. It became clear that, such maps were kept in the Great Library of Alexandria located in Egypt before being annihilated by the Crusaders in VII century".

All these facts prove that, cartography is one of the most ancient science branches and there were professional cartogramphers - authors of exact maps even 15000 years ago. Afterwards mentioned maps began to be spread in new civilization centers of the world.

Books full of rich historical facts and sensational information will be interesting for scientists all over the world and attract special attention. Discovery of America and Brazil is the most interesting part of the history of geographical discoveries and these books are significant source for deep investigation of mentioned theme.

Scientific works of Ramiz Daniz may be spread among scientists and ordinary readers interested in the history of geographical discoveries. Ramiz Daniz has found out new facts and so could destroy stereotypes concerning this field.

Ramiz Mammadov – Laureate of State Prize
Associate Member of the Academy of Science,
doctor of technical sciences, director of the Institute
of Geography of the Academy of Science

The sensational map found in the
Topkapi Palace Museum of Istanbul

The admiral Piri ibn Haji Mammad Reis (1475-1554) was an experienced captain, talented navigator, skilful navy captain, well-known navy commander, professional navigator officer and educated cartographer of his time. His maps were the most necessary aids for the science of navigation. Besides it, Piri Reis could combine different maps, which had different scales, in one map. All captains and navigator officers wanted to have such maps.

German scientists – Professors Gustav Adolf Deissmann and Paul Kohl found an ancient map drawn on the pergament made of the gazelle skin when they carried out restoration works in the Topkapi Palace Museum of Istanbul in 1929. That map was made in Chelibolu in the month of Muharram of 919th year of the Islamic calendar (1513).

Piri Reis made an atlas in 1528 and included this map in that atlas by fixing the date as 1513. Afterwards it turned out that, mentioned historical material was copied from ancient manuscripts kept in the library of Constantinople.

After reading about the discovery of the map in the Illustrated London News, the Secretary of State of the United States, Henry L. Stimson, contacted United States Ambassador to Turkey Charles Sherryl and asked for an investigation to find the original Columbus map. He suggested that the *"Columbus map"* should be somewhere in Turkey. However, despite the full assistance provided by the Turkish authorities, no results were achieved.

The map shows a large number of positioning lines drawn from the center between Africa and South America, probably for better navigation accuracy, which is not typical of the preserved maps of that time. Even maps created decades later cannot boast such accuracy in maintaining proportions.

Most cartographers, geographers and historians of Europe did their best for being in that library, but couldn't achieve it. Libraries of Pergamum, Babylonia, Alexandria, Baghdad, Tabriz, Maragha, Damascus and Athens were moved to Istanbul during wars. Everybody knew that, there were a lot of ancient manuscripts, maps, anthropological and ethnographical information in mentioned library and it was possible to get sensational information by getting acquainted with them. Piri Reis's map, where outlines of the Western Hemisphere were described, was one of such materials.

According to historical sources, Piri Reis often visited that library in order to analyze ancient documents and maps. Mentioned map could attract attention of Turkish scientists for its exactness. It was almost the first map, which described outlines of America. Besides it, the sensational material included outlines of North America and Antarctica. It was made 21 years after the first travel of Columbus. But the Genoese admiral hadn't visited the continent besides eastern coasts of Panama, Nicaragua and Honduras. Antarctica was discovered after more than 300 years by Fadday Bellingshausen and Mikhail Lazarev (1820). That's why most scientists made radical steps in order to analyze the map. Author of the map and date of its preparation were interesting for them.

Piri Reis had copied lines from other ancient maps and included notes of Columbus made during his travel in his map. The Turkish admiral admitted that, he had copied western part from Christopher Columbus's map. It means that, the well-known traveler had unique maps, which stimulated his first travel. It should be taken into consideration that, historians and geographers carried out unsuccessful researches during hundreds of years in accordance with *"Columbus's lost map"* made by Columbus in West End islands.

There is no doubt that, the map found in the Topkapi Palace Museum of Istanbul by Adolf Deissmann and Paul Kohl was a sensational discovery. It wasn't similar to maps made at the end of XV century and XVI century. Though necessary devices and equipments didn't exist then, coordinates of South America and Africa had been determined exactly. Could such map be made by any well-known cartographer, geographer or sea traveler of Europe? German and Turkish scientists investigated found map attentively.

The American secretary of state Henry Stimson also was interested in this investigation. He thought that, *"Columbus's map"* could be in Turkey. He ordered the ambassador of USA in Turkey to start researches in order to find mentioned map. Though the Turkish government supported researches comprehensively, any success couldn't be achieved.

Piri Reis mentioned that, he had used about twenty maps made during the age of Macedonian Alexandre in accordance with exact calculations. But scientists didn't believe his explanation about the map found in 1929.

Scientists couldn't believe the Turkish admiral's statements as aerocosmic technology didn't exist then. There wasn't any copy of maps made during the age of Macedonian Alexandre. The Turkish admiral's map caused great resonance in Turkey.

The map was published in many editions in the state publishing house in 1935 in accordance with the order of the president of Turkey Mustafa Kamala Ataturk, who was proud that, cartography had been developed in Turkey even in XVI century.

Experts of the USA and especially captain Arlington X. Mueller, who was considered professional expert in the fields of cartography and navigation analyzed mentioned map in 50s years of XX century and get sensetional result. The coastline of the Queen Maud Land covered in ice had been described in the southern part of the map. Probably, the map was made when mentioned territory wasn't covered in ice. Of course, this sensetional result amazed experts.

As opponents of Mueller didn't accept his result, he resorted to help of the director of Weston observatory attached to Boston College Daniel L. Lainhen and director of the observatory attached to Georgetown University Francis Hayden for verification of his result. Mentioned experts participated in the radio discussion made on August 26, 1956 on this theme. The theme was spread all over the world. After it, the Professor of Kinsk College located in New Hampshire Charles H. Hapgood began to be interested in mentioned theme. The map was included in the program of scientific investigations of Kin-State College owing to his efforts.

After long investigations, Ch. Hapgood sent request to the technical-intelligence escadrille of the cartography department number 8 of Air Forces of the USA. Joint work lasted for more than two years and it was proved that mentioned map had been made before the Queen Maud Land was covered in ice.

Dear Professor Hepgood!

Your request to evaluate some unusual details on a 1513 Pee Reis map has been reviewed. The claim that the lower part of the map depicts the coast of Princess Maud, Queen Maud, Antarctica, and the Palmer Peninsula is reasonable. We believe that this conclusion is the most logical and most likely correct interpretation of the map.

In the lower part of the map, the geographical elements show very noticeable similarities to the seismic scanning data of the Swedish-British Antarctic expedition of 1959 on the real geologic relief under the glacier there. This indicates that the coast was mapped before it was covered with ice. The glacier in this region today is about a mile thick.

We have no idea how the data on this map can correlate with the expected level of geographic knowledge in 1513.

After two years of working together, it was finally proved that this part of the map was drawn before the mainland ices. Based on the version that the map actually depicts the ice-free coast of Antarctica, as noted in Olmeer's letter above, it could only have been mapped during the preglacial period, as the glacier extends far beyond the land and visibly changes the shape of the continent. According to modern thinking, the ice sheet on the surface of Antarctica formed a few million years ago and the continent has never been completely free of ice since then. But the age of man as a biological species does not exceed hundreds of thousands of years, human civilization - a few millennia. If even to accept a hypothesis about some prehistoric "cartographers" who lived millions years ago, it remains unclear how the results of their works got to people, because the most ancient known civilizations (Egyptian and Sumerian) appeared no more than 6000 years ago.

There are two main differences from the known coastlines: the North American coast mentioned above and the southern part of the South American shores. Admiral Piri Reis's map shows the last one curving sharply eastward, starting in today's Rio de Janeiro. A more popular interpretation of the area was to identify this section with the Queen of Maud Coast Land (Antarctica). This statement is usually associated with Arlington H. Mahler, a civil engineer and amateur archaeologist who was a supporter of pre-Columbian trans-Pacific hypotheses. Although his claims were not well received by scholars, they were revived in Charles Hapgood's 1966 book **"Maps of Ancient Sea Kings"**. This book presents the theory of the global study of preclassical undiscovered civilization, based on an analysis of this and other ancient and late medieval maps. It is better known that these statements were repeated in the **"Chariots of the Gods"** by Erich von Daniken (who attributed the knowledge of the coast to foreigners) and

1421 by Gavin Menzis: **"The Year China Discovered the World,"** both of which were widely condemned by both scholars.

A more sober analysis of these claims was published by cartography historian Gregory Mackintosh, who examined the map in detail in his 1513 book, **"The Peerie Reis Map"**.[1] He was able to find sources for much of the map in Columbus' works. He explained some features (such as the appearance of the Virgin Islands in two places) by using several maps as sources; others (such as errors in North American geography). As for the exact description of the proposed Antarctic coast, there are two notable errors.

First, it is shown hundreds of kilometres north of its proper location; second, the Drake Strait is completely absent and the Antarctic peninsula is supposedly connected to the west coast of Patagonia. The identification of this area on the map with the cold Antarctic coast is also difficult to link to the map notes that describe the region with its warm climate.

Afterwards Ch. Hapgood continued investigations independently and got the next sensational result.

---

[1] Athens and London: University of Georgia Press, 2000.

Latitudes of popular islands located near Antarctica had been fixed on the map in detail. Probably, they were found by means of maps made before by applying modern spherecal trigonometry. It is obvious that, authors of the map knew that, the Earth was spherical and they knew the Earth's length with 50 miles error.

Several optimist sea travelers believed existence of **"Southern land"** in the middle of XVI century. One of them was well-known Spanish seaman, architect and annalist Pedro Sarmiento de Gamboa, who defended that idea even before publication of popular **"Atlas"** of Gerhard Mercator. The well-known Spanish sea traveler Alvaro de Mendana de Neyra organized expedition towards the south of the Pacific Ocean in accordance with his offer in order to find the mythical country Ophir located in the south of the Earth.

...Mendana saw atoll or reef (Ontong Java or Rocador) on February 1, 1568 and approached **"large land"** separated from the ocean with coral reeves (Santa Isabel) on February 7... Mendana thought that, he had discovered Ophir in the southern continent (the king Solomon had sent vessels to Ophir to find gold in order to decorate Jerusalem temple in the myth). But he had discovered archipelago, which was named Solomon Islands.[1]

All coordinates were restored in accordance with investigations carried out by American architects and cartographers Blanche, Mueller and Walter. It turns out that, coastlines of the Old World, New World and Antarctica were described on the map exactly. The coastline of Antarctica wasn't covered in ice in 11-4 thousand BC. It means that, cartography had developed 6 thousand years ago as highly as the present time. Besides the eastern coast of South America, the western coast and Ant Mountains also were described on the map of admiral Piri Reis.

Research carried out by the American Nero-Cartographers Blanche, Mellery and Walter has restored all the correct map coordinates. It turned out that not only the contours of the Old and New World, the Arctic regions and Antarctica were marked with high accuracy. For example:

- The boundaries of Queen Maud's Earth were precisely marked;

[1] Daniz R. The scientist passed ahead of centuries – Nasiraddin Tusi. Lap Lambert Academic Publishing", Riqa. 2019. 302-303 p.

- An inexplicably correct image of South America and the Andes in the Western Continent;

- The Amazon River is depicted quite correctly;

- The Falkland Islands are depicted at their correct latitude (they were not known until 1592);

- A large island in the Antarctic Ocean, east of the South American coast, is depicted. This island is depicted, just above the underwater meridian of the Mid-Atlantic Ridge, above the tiny rocks of Saints Peter and Paul.

Sensational maps of Antarctica

Despite numerous claims of extreme accuracy, Gregory McIntosh compared the Pierry Reis map with several other maps of the epoch and discovered that the Pierry Reis map of the world was not the most accurate map of the sixteenth century, as claimed. There were other world maps that were slightly more accurate than this. For example, the Ribeiro maps of the 1520s and 1530s, the Ortelius map of 1570, and the Wright Prayer map of 1599 ("the best map of the sixteenth century") are just better known examples.

Mackintosh's position is understandable, but it is not clear that he compares a map drawn in 1513 with maps of 1570 and 1599. That is, the Ribeiro map was produced in 15-25 years, the Ortelius map in 57 years, and the Wright Molinje map in 86 years after the Turkish admiral's map. It must be admitted that after 1515, most cities in Europe, where cartography was rapidly developing, began to produce maps with contours of the Caribbean, eastern Brazil, and North America. And 15 years later, cartographers and navigators had access to the contours of the western part of the isthmus of Panama and the banks of present-day Colombia, Ecuador, Peru, and northern Chile, plus the banks of the Strait of Magellan.

The work of Piri Reis is not to be compared to that of the aforementioned cartographers, who found it easier to acquire the nose material for making maps than the Turkish admiral. Because they were Europeans, and Piri Reis was a citizen of the Ottoman Turkey, to whom almost all European countries were hostile.

The well-known Flemish cartographer Abraham Ortelius described **"Southern land"** in the southern part of the Pacific and Indian Oceans on his map *"Theatre of the world"* consisted of 53 maps. This idea was supported by another well-known Flemish cartographer Gerhard Mercator, who described **"Southern land"** in his atlas.[1]

This fact caused all scientists to think. How could the Turkish admiral describe mentioned places exactly? There is no doubt that, mentioned map wasn't made by Piri Reis only. Who was the real author of the map and when was it made?

Ch. Hapgood came to the following conclusion when analyzed the map: "Exact information is exchanged between nations. The map was made by unknown nation and was found by Phoenicians and Creteans, who were considered genius seamen during more than thousand years, in ancient times. It became clear that, such maps were kept in the Great Library of Alexandria located in Egypt before being annihilated by the Crusaders in VII century".[1]

The ancient Greek scientist Fukidid wrote: "The most famous tsar of Creteans Minos had established navy and

[1] Daniz R. The scientist passed ahead of centuries – Nasiraddin Tusi. Lap Lambert Academic Publishing", Riqa. 2019. 303 p.
[1] Ч. Хепгуд. Древние карты морских королей.

occupied large part of the Ellyn Sea and Kirkland Islands".[2] As if they were in a hurry. Other nations living around the Mediterranean Sea couldn't use navigation, vessels and maps as professionally as they did. But their appearing and disappearing were very enigmatic. It is known that, they lost their hegemony in the Sea of Crete in 1150 BC, when Doris moved to Peloponnesian Peninsula.[1]

Almost everybody knew that, Phoenicians were skilful seamen. They systematically sailed to the Atlantic Ocean from the Strait of Gibraltar and investigated coasts of Europe and Africa. Phoenicians used ancient maps for sailing in the ocean safely.

Most researchers wrote that, Piri Reis's map was used by other cartographers too. It means that, those maps were kept in Alexandria in several copies. They were spread all over the world after Egypt was occupied. Descriptions of Antarctica also were spread in several countries. I think, Gerhard Mercator, Oronteus Fineus and Philipp Buache also had such maps.

[2] Фукидид. История. I том, Москва, 1915. стр. 5.
[1] Хульмут Ханке. Люди, корабли, океаны. Москва, «Прогресс», 1984. стр. 33.

Some scientists including Ch. Hapgood wrote that, sensational maps made by above mentioned experts were kept in the Library of Alexandria and were taken to the library of the Byzantine Empire afterwards together with other documents. Probably, most copies of mentioned maps were taken to Venetia in 1204 owing to Venetian seamen. But nobody can surely mention that, that material was given to the Turkish admiral by Venetian seamen or merchants.

It couldn't happen as there was a war between Ottoman Empire and Venetia. All these facts prove that, cartography is one of the most ancient science branches and there were professional cartogramphers – authors of exact maps even 15000 years ago. Afterwards mentioned maps began to be spread in new civilization centers of the world.

Activities and wide knowledge of the Turkish admiral

Ancient maps were kept in well-known libraries of Alexandria owing to Phoenicians and Creteans.

Babylonia was one of ancient civilization centers of the world before the ancient time. The most talented experts, well-known scientists and wise persons had gathered there.

Probably, maps of other parts of Antarctica and the whole Earth were taken to Babylonia by unknown people during unknown civilization. Afterwards Macedonian Alexandre started his marches in order to conquer the world and declared Babylonia center of his empire founded at the beginning of IV century BC. The conqueror of the world founded Alexandria in 332 BC in Egypt and it became one of scientific and cultural centers of the ancient time during a very short time. So, ancient maps kept in Babylonia began to be moved to the famous library of Alexandria. That's why the admiral Piri Reis mentioned that, those maps had been made during the age of Alexandre.

One of annalists, who lived during the age of Alexandre, Vitruvius wrote: "Isgandar saw the real port near the settlement of fishermen Rakotis located near Faros Island, between the Mediterranean Sea and Lake Mariut when he reached the rank of the Nile River. Alexandre ordered the architect Deinocrat, who accompanied him during marches, to establish a town in the place, where they went". Really, Deinocrat established large town there during a very short time and gold sarcophagus of Alexandre were brought to that town after ten years.

Though Alexandria was very young, it could become scientific and cultural center of the ancient world. Well-known scientists and philosophers of all countries located around the Mediterranean Sea visited that town. The town was famous for its magnificent library, Temple of Muses and Academy of Sciences.[1]

Scientists gathered in the temple, worked on manuscripts kept in the library of Alexandria and kept several copies of their works there. There are a lot of similarities between Maragha observatory and Temple of Muses. It is necessary to analyze this fact.

The most progressive period of the temple was during the age of Ptolemy Everget III. He used to buy original manuscripts and could get articles of Eschil, Sofokl and Euripid by convincing Athenians... So, about 200000 manuscripts were collected in the temple during the age of Ptolemy and his heirs continued his mission afterwards.

---

[1] М. Гумилевская. Как открывали мир. Москва, «Д.Л», 1977. стр. 38.

Number of manuscripts kept in the temple grew significantly after the library of Pergamum was moved to Alexandria and became 700000. There were hundreds and thousands of manuscripts among them and most of them were spread in most cities of the world...

The poet Callimachus was the head of the temple after Demetrius of Pharia. He was a poet and scientist. Callimachus had created 120-volume *"Catalogue of the library of Alexandria"*, which resembled encyclopedia of history and culture, there.[1] But the temple had a very tragic ending.

Tsaritsa of Egypt Cleopatra moved manuscripts to the Temple of Serapes in 48 BC in order to save them. The consul of Rome Gaius Julius Caesar ordered to burn part of manuscripts in the port when he came to Alexandria in order to prevent rebellion.

Subsequently, the library building was restored, and (according to one version) Mark Anthony added to its collection at the expense of the other largest library of the Hellenistic world - the Per-Hama Library.

---

[1] Н. А. Ионина, автор-составитель. Сто великих чудес света. Москва, «Вече», 2000. стр. 146,148.

In 216, Caracalla gave Alexandria to rob soldiers, which could also damage the safety of books.

In 273 the Roman Emperor Aurelian destroyed and burned the library during the capture of Alexandria, suppressing the riot of Queen Zenobia.

In IV century the part of survived books has been taken out to Constantinople.

In 391, there were disturbances and conflicts between pagans and Christians in the city. Eventually, Patriarch Theophilus of Alexandria received permission to destroy pagan temples, which led to the destruction of Serapium.

There is an opinion, which goes back to the work of **"Chronicon Syriacum" of the** thirteenth century Syrian Bishop Gregory Bar Ebray, that the surviving remains of manuscripts died in the 7th-8th centuries under the rule of Muslim Arabs.

The famous historian of the Caliphate V.O. Bolshakov writes: "However, neither John of Nikius, who reported a lot of pogroms and robberies during the Arab conquest, nor any other Christian historian hostile to Islam, mentions the fire of the bibliopoeque".

Thus, it is difficult to attribute the loss of the library to a specific event or to blame it definitively on heathens, Christians or Muslims. There is no unanimity on this point. For example, Plutarch vinyled Caesar, Edward Gibbon vinyled Christians, Gregory Bar-Hebrew vinyled Muslims, and the authors of the Encyclopedia Britannica place the main blame on Aurelian.

In a word, most of the invaluable sources of knowledge gathered there have died.

But some of the materials were still taken out of the country.

So, great part of valuable sources, which were collected during several centuries, was annihilated there. But some of them were taken abroad.

Expeditions were organized towards the coastline of Africa hundreds of years ago and surely, successful travels were realized owing to made maps. Seamen, who lived on coasts of Egypt, Levant and Arabian Peninsula, were considered the most skilful experts. Probably, some of maps made during that period were kept in libraries of the ancient time and scientists used those materials in their scientific works. Arabs organized successful expeditions around the Indian Ocean and Phoenicians could do it on eastern coasts of the Atlantic Ocean.

The exact date of his birth is unknown. His father's name was Hacı Mehmed Piri. The honorary and informal Islamic title Hadji (Turkish - Haci) in Piri's and his father's names indicate that they both had completed the Hajj (Islamic pilgrimage) by going to Mecca during the dedicated annual period.

Piri began engaging in government-supported privateering (a common practice in the Mediterranean Sea among both the Muslim and Christian states of the 15th and 16th centuries) when he was young, following his uncle Kemal Reis, a well-known corsair and seafarer of the time, who later became a famous admiral of the Ottoman Navy. During this period, together with his uncle, he took part in many naval wars of the Ottoman Empire against Spain, the Republic of Genoa and the Republic of Venice, including the First Battle of Lepanto (Battle of Zonchio) in 1499 and the Second Battle of Lepanto (Battle of Modon) in 1500. When his uncle Kemal Reis died in 1511 (his ship was wrecked by a storm in the Mediterranean Sea, while he was heading to Egypt), Piri returned to Gelibolu, where he started working on his studies about navigation.

During this period Piri Reis saw many countries and described all the ports and bays in detail. He lived during the reign of three sultans.

His public service began during the reign of Sultan Bayezid II (1481-1512), covered the entire period of the reign of Sultan Selim I Yavuz (1512-1520) and part of the reign of Suleiman Kanuni (1520-1566).[1]

By 1516, he was again at sea as a ship captain in the Ottoman fleet. He took part in the 1516-1517 Ottoman conquest of Egypt. In 1522 he participated in the Siege of Rhodes against the Knights of St. John, which ended with the island's surrender to the Ottomans on 25 December 1522 and the permanent departure of the Knights from Rhodes on 1 January 1523 (the Knights relocated briefly to Sicily and later permanently to Malta). In 1524 he captained the ship that took the Ottoman Grand Vizier Pargalı İbrahim Pasha Grand to Egypt.

Surviving fragment of the second World Map of Piri Reis (1528)

In 1547, Piri had risen to the rank of Reis (admiral) as the Commander of the Ottoman Fleet in the Indian Ocean and Admiral of the Fleet in Egypt, headquartered in Suez. On 26 February 1548 he recaptured Aden from the Portuguese, followed in 1552 by the Muscat, which Portugal had occupied since 1507, and the strategically

---

[1] Reyes P. Kitab-e-Bahriye. Translation from Old Ottoman language, compilation and foreword by Aliyeva Taira. Baku: Ecoprint, 2019.

important island of Kish. Turning further east, Piri Reis attempted to capture the island of Hormuz in the Strait of Hormuz, at the entrance of the Persian Gulf, unsuccessfully. When the Portuguese turned their attention to the Persian Gulf, Piri Reis occupied the Qatar peninsula to deprive the Portuguese of suitable bases on the Arabian coast.

He then returned to Egypt, an old man approaching the age of 90. When he refused to support the Ottoman Vali (Governor) of Barsa, Kubad Pasha, in another campaign against the Portuguese in the northern Persian Gulf, Piri Reis was beheaded in 1553.

Several warships and submarines of the Turkish Navy have been named after Piri Reis.

There were a lot of maps made by Arabs and Piri Reis learned most of those maps. Portuguese used materials of Arabs and especially well-known seaman and skilful navigator Ahmad ibn Majid when sailed from the Atlantic Ocean to southern coasts of Africa. He had sailed to the south of Africa together with Bartolommeo Dias and to India together with Vasco da Gama (as a navigation officer). It is known that, Ahmad ibn Majid was a professional seaman and had learned this profession by means of corresponding documents. He had described his knowledge in about 40 scientific works and two books – *"Collection of main principles about seas"* (1462) and *"Book about bases and laws of navigation"* (1490).

Those materials were often used by Piri Reis as they were spread in several countries. Piri Reis got acquainted with several parts of *"Hatainame"* after M. Polo in order to expand his knowledge. The Ottoman traveler Ali Akbar Hatai was in that country in 1505-1506 when the emperor of Chine Chu Kou Chao came to the throne and he published mentioned book in Persian in Istanbul in 1520.

Besides it, the Turkish admiral had read scientific works of the most famous geographers and astronomers of Europe including Toscanelli. It means that, Piri Reis was enough educated and didn't fall behind other geographers and cartographers.

"Kitab-i Bahriye" ("Book of the Seas")

It is known that, Piri Reis was a head admiral of Egypt and had great competencies. As he ruled the Mediterranean Sea and especially the territory between the center and eastern coasts, he could control many routes. As vessels sailing from France and Spain to kingdoms located in the Apennine Peninsula and cities of Greece, from Venetia, Genoa and Naples to France, Spain and cities of Greece were controlled, they were often attacked by the navy of Piri Reis. Besides it, his spies gathered important information about expeditions, which sailed from the Mediterranean Sea and ports of Portugal, Spain, France, Netherlands and England, and sent gathered materials to Piri Reis.

Thus, the admiral had a lot of secret materials about kingdoms of Europe. Piri Reis wrote his *"Book of navigation" ("Kitab-i Bahriye"),* which had a significant role in the field of navigation, owing to mentioned materials.

"Kitab-i Bahriyeh (Book of the Seas) is one of the most famous books of navigation. The book contains detailed information on major ports, bays, bays, capes, peninsulas, islands, straits in the Mediterranean Sea, as well as methods of navigation and navigation-based information on astronomy. The book also contains information about the local life of each country and city, as well as interesting aspects of their culture. **"Kitab-i Bahriyeh** was originally written between 1511 and 1521, but was revised with additional information and better maps between 1524 and 1525 in order to be presented as a gift to Suleiman the Magnificent. The revised 1525 edition contains a total of 434 pages and 290 maps.

By the production of **"Kitab-i Bahriyeh" ("Book of moswimming")** Piri Reis entered the galaxy of forever living celebrities. In 1521-1525, he was a member of the tribe of living celebrities.

The second section begins with a description of the Strait of Dardanelles and continues with the islands and coasts of the Aegean, Ionian, Adriatic, Tyrrheanian, Ligurian, French Riviera, Balearic Islands, Spanish coast, Strait of Gibraltar, Canary Islands, North African coast, Egypt and the Nile, Levanta, and Anatolia coasts. This section also includes descriptions and drawings of the famous monuments and buildings in each city, as well as biographical information about Pyri Reis himself, where he also explains why he prefers to collect these schemata in books rather than in a single map that could not fit so much information and detail.

The cards are made of gazelle leather pieces measuring 90 x 63 cm, 86 x 60 cm, 90 x 65 cm, 85 x 60 cm, 87 x 63 cm and 86 x 62 cm.

Piri Reis repeatedly complemented it, increased the number of individual maps included in the book, accompanied by comments and through Damat Ibrahim Pasha gave it to Sultan Suleyman the Magnificent.

For this reason, the lists of **Kitab-i Bahriyeh,** found both in Turkey and elsewhere in the world, are based on two foundations (927 and 932 AH). No autographs have been found. According to some sources, the autograph of the work written in 1525 was purchased by the French National Bibliotheca.

Most of the lists are in Turkey (in the libraries of Aya Sofia, Topkapi, Maritime Museum, etc.), while others are outside Turkey (Dresden, Bologna (Nos. 3612, 3613), (London, Oxford Bibliotheca), (Paris, Nos. 220, 965, National Bibliotheca, Vienna, Berlin). Another list was recently discovered in Hungary (Torok, F.24). The oldest list, transcribed in 1544, is kept in Drezdene. The work was translated and republished more than once by different authors. One of the translations of this book is a brief translation made in 1756 by a translator of the Foreign Office and the French Royal Bibliotheque D. D. Cardonet under the title **"Le flambeau de la Mйditerranйe"**. It was not, however, published. The manuscript of this translation is kept at the Bibliothique Nationale de Paris (Catalogue No.:F.F.22279). Professor Paul Cahle of the University of Bonn translated **"Bahriye"** into German. The book, together with a Turkish text, was published in Germany in 1926.

The first facsimile of the book **"Bahriyeh"** was published in Turkey in 1935 with explanations and comments. It was republished in 2002. The foreword was written by Haidar Al-pagut, a teacher at the Naval Academy, and Fevzi Kurtoglu, a teacher at the Naval Lyceum. The index was compiled by naval reserve officer Fehmi Pekol. In 1973, a translation of the work into modern Turkish by retired colonel Yavuz Selimoglu was published in two volumes. The preface was written by the Army Admiral, Commander of the Naval Forces Kemal Cayacan and Mehmet Onder. In 1988, the book **"Bahriyeh"** was published in four volumes simultaneously in Old Ottoman, Turkish and English. The authors of the Turkish text are Vahid 3abuk, Tyulay Duran, and the English text are Robert Bragner. The author of the foreword is Mert Bayat, a member of the Naval Academy, Colonel of Staff".

The book begins with the praise of Allah, the Prophet Muhammad (as), his family, his companions, as well as the three sultans in whose time Piri Reis lived and worked. The reason for writing the book is set out below. The poetic part, consisting of 972 bayts (double) and divided into 23 chapters, is beautifully composed. The first chapter explains natural phenomena. Here Piri Reis tells about the travels and military campaigns he made with his uncle Kemal Reis, etc. The second chapter encourages sailors to study the science of the sea perfectly, mentions the great commander Alexander the Great, describes the death of Kemal Reyes, etc.

Especially interesting is the twenty-third chapter, which describes the activities of Columbus and Alexander Makedonsky. There Piri Reis tells about the discovery of the Antilles (America). In this chapter, Pirie Reis says that he had the map used by Columbus and that in discovering America, Columbus knew where he was going thanks to a book that fell into his hands. Pirie Reis writes: "In the hands of the astronomer Columbus of Genoa fell into the hands of a book left by Alexander the Great. This book contained all the information about the science of navigation. Christopher Columbus read it and, guided by this book, found the Antilles". Then he explains how Alexander the Great traveled around the world and about all heard, ordered to write and compile books. These books were kept in Egypt. Over time, Europeans moved to Egypt. However, when Egypt was conquered by Amr Bin As many people from the nobles fled to the European countries, taking with them the abovementioned books of Alexander. Later, the Europeans translated them into their own languages. The translator was Bartholomew. According to Piri Reis, based on this knowledge, Europeans discovered many countries.

This book was translated from Old Ottoman language by Tair Aliyeva. This is what she writes: ...The work of Piri Reis, a great Turkish scientist, navigator, cartographerfa, admiral of the Ottoman Navy of the 16th century, is a masterpiece in the field of world history, geography and navigation. Pyri Reis is renowned for his work in geography, cartography and instructions in maritime navigation. He produced his first map of the world with a text attachment in 1513 and completed the second map in 1528. The book of the highly respected admiral of the Turkish Maritime Service, written by him in 1521, "exemplifies the great service of both navigation and world history as a whole, and is an authentic document attesting to the extent to which Turkish navigation reached the Atlantic Ocean in the 16th century.[1]

Piri Reis was mostly interested in maps describing outlines of important geographical points, especially unknown coastlines and he made his future plans in accordance with them. That's why he was considered the most skilful and experienced navy leader.

As Egypt was the colony of the Ottoman Empire, most historical documents kept there were taken to Istanbul. The Turkish admiral, who was interested in historical documents and different maps, found a lot of maps in Alexandria and Istanbul, worked on them and made his perfect atlas in 1528. But one of those maps could attract attention of modern scientists. It was the map, which was made in 1513 and described outlines of America, Antarctica and North-western Africa.

Piri Reis admitted that, he had made that map by copying several ancient maps. His admission made

---

[1] Reyes P. Kitab-e-Bahriye. Translation from Old Ottoman language, compilation and foreword by Aliyeva Taira. Baku: Ecoprint, 2019.

works of researchers easier and they could carry out systematic works in this field.

Who is the real author of the map - admiral Piri Reis or Nasiraddin Tusi?

Cartographers and historians wondered how the Turkish admiral could find the most notable map of XX century. As it was mentioned above, Piri Reis wrote that, he had made western part of the map according to notes made by Columbus on the map he used during his first travel.

The American secretary of state Henry Stimson, who tried to find the origin of *"Columbus's lost map"*, thought that, it was in Turkey. Of course, most scientists agreed with this thought. Even if Piri Reis used "Columbus's lost map", he had found it in an unknown situation. Probably, the Turkish admiral was obliged to keep mentioned map in one of strategic buildings of Istanbul as a historical document after using it. It means that, doubts of Henry Stimson weren't groundless. But long-term researches were unsuccessful. Either those researches weren't organized as well as necessary, or their participants weren't professional experts.

Several important questions appear: First, who were real authors of manuscripts found by Piri Reis? Second, did Columbus have an original copy of the map (the part describing America and West Africa) during his first travel? Then, how could the Turkish admiral find mentioned map? Third, how could the Turkish admiral find mentioned map? It is obvious that, the sea traveler couldn't be the author of the mysterious map. Outlines of the New World discovered by him in 1492 were drawn in mentioned map before the expedition left Spain. Fourth, who is the real author of the map and how could he determine corresponding outlines and coordinates? Fifth, how could the map appear in the Topkapi Palace Museum of Istanbul and why weren't historians, geographers and cartographers aware of its existence until it was found in 1929. What was the reason?

According to historical sources, Piri Reis usually spent a lot of time in the library of the Empire in order to analyze ancient documents and maps. The map, which described outlines exactly, attracted attention of Turkish scientists. That map was one of the first maps, which described outlines of America (for the first time, outlines of America were drawn by Juan de la Cosa in 1500 and then by Cantino in 1502). Besides it, the map included outlines of North America and Antarctica. It turns out that, Columbus's lost map was in Istanbul. It is possible to understand it by looking at pictures of vessels drawn on the map.

1. There were caravels, carracks and naos in the western part of the map, though Piri Reis's navy consisted of galeras, galeas, fusts and other vessels. So, the author wanted to mention that, there was an unknown continent between Eastern Asia and Western Europe and that continent was discovered by Spaniards.

2. Mentioned pictures of vessels prove admiral Piri Reis's supposition about *"Columbus's map"*. The Genoese admiral had used caravels, carracks and naos when he travelled to coasts of the New World and proved that those vessels were important during long ocean passages.

Coastlines described on the mysterious map are noteworthy. They prove that, maps describing outlines of the Earth existed in ancient times. One fact also should be mentioned. As there weren't aerocosmic technologies then, scientists didn't believe statements of the Turkish admiral. None of maps made during the age of Isgandar has remained until present time. It is known that, Isgandar returned to Mesopotamia with the help of the commander of his navy Nearh after his march to India. The navy didn't meet with difficulties during the travel. It has been mentioned in works of Arius and Strabo.

The Greek merchant, traveler and geographer from Massalia by name Pifey left his motherland and started his travel in 325 BC, when troops of Isgandar returned to Greece. He used very difficult route and reached British Isles, some coasts of North Europe including Tule Island (was described on the map of Eratosthenes) and Baltic Sea. That travel was described in Pifey's book *"About the ocean"*. Though mentioned book hasn't remained until present time, Strabo and Pliny the Elder gave enough information by basing on it. If the Greek traveler hadn't corresponding map, he couldn't achieve success in such difficult travel. Thus, there were a lot of maps describing most territories of the Earth during the age of Isgandar and Pifey had used those maps. It shouldn't be forgotten that, Phoenicians, who were considered skilful seamen, had travelled from the Strait of Gibraltar towards the north and south.

1. Hapgood wrote that, the map was made by an unknown nation and most of maps made in ancient times were gathered and analyzed in the library of Alexandria.[1]

It was necessary to know navigation, spherical trigonometry, astronomy, mathematics, trigonometry, geography and cartography in order prepare such material. Seamen and travelers couldn't know these fields.

2. Only skilful scientist could combine several maps in the world map. He had to know mathematical and spherical trigonometry. All scientists of the world knew that, the inventor of mathematical and spherical trigonometry was Tusi (not Regiomontanus). I think the original of the map (without the part describing Antarctica) could be made by Tusi.

3. The Turkish admiral's navy had worked in the Mediterranean Sea and he was in Spain. Was he aware of existence of Columbus's map?

He could find such map in Istanbul either. As I mentioned above, scientists of Maragha observatory could make several maps describing outlines of America. Nasiraddin Tusi, Muayyidaddin Ordy, Gutbaddin Shirazi

---

[1] Ч. Хепгуд «Древние карты морских королей».

and Chinese scientist Fao Mun-Chi could have such maps as they had important posts in the observatory.

Probably, Gutbaddin Shirazi took his map to Alexandria when he went to Egypt as the ambassador of Mongols and afterwards the map was taken to the capital of the Ottoman Empire by means of Turks. It turns out that, Columbus wasn't aware of existence of the map kept in Istanbul, so, he couldn't find it.

Then, how and where could the Spanish admiral find *"Columbus's lost map"?* I have found only one answer: The Chinese scientist of Maragha observatory Fao Mun-Chi took the map made in the observatory to his motherland in 1267. According to previous chapters, Marco Polo had taken that map to Italy. It was kept in the library leaded by Toscanelli in Florentine and Columbus got acquainted with it there.

4. How were outlines and coordinates determined? It is known that, mentioned map was made in accordance with several manuscripts. I'll describe history of the part describing the north of Antarctica.

Nasiraddin Tusi worked in Alexandria and carried out interesting investigations in most educational, scientific and cultural centers located there, besides working in famous cities and educational centers of the Near East.

Most works and historical documents kept in the library of Alexandria were taken to the capital of the Byzantine Empire after the library of Alexandria was annihilated by Crusaders (X century). Besides it, Nasiraddin Tusi got good opportunities for expanding his scientific activity after annihilation of the Baghdad Caliphate by Hulegu khan in 1258. A grandiose library was established in Baghdad during the age of Abbasids and it was full of valuable works. Those works were brought to the capital of the Caliphate from occupied cities including Alexandria.

Tusi also used those works in order to expand his knowledge. Probably, the scientist had found several parts of mentioned map, which would be known as *"Admiral Piri Reis's map"* in future, in Baghdad and started to investigate that historical document before foundation of Maragha observatory (1259). Europe, Asia and Africa (of course, partially) had already been investigated until the middle of XIII century.

Study of a geographical map and
some results of scientists

The sensational conclusion of Charles Hapgood about the map was as following: "Latitudes of well-known islands located near Antarctica were described on the map in detail. Probably, those results were achieved in accordance with an older map made by using modern spherical trigonometry. It is obvious that, authors of the map knew that, the Earth was spherical and they knew the Earth's length with 50 miles error".

I think Tusi had an important role in this achievement. It was difficult to combine coordinates fixed on the map made 6000 years ago with modern coordinates. It is known that, Nasiraddin Tusi and scientists of Maragha observatory knew spherical trigonometry enough well. Probably, the Azerbaijani scientist had found the map without the coordinate system.

Nasiraddin Tusi fixed geographic latitudes and longitudes as he knew spherical trigonometry. Skilful seamen could determine approximate distance between two points located on the ocean after analyzing the map.

So, Columbus knew how long he had to travel during his first travel owing to mentioned map. Some modern scientists also accept this hypothesis. There wasn't any other skilful scientist, who knew astronomy, mathematics and geography enough well and was able to fix geographic latitudes and longitudes exactly, before Columbus found the map.

As it is known, Piri Reis's map included only description of the western part of the Earth. It should be mentioned that, Nasiraddin Tusi had determined coordinates of 256 cities including cities of Spain and Chine. I think the Azerbaijani scientist had that map without the part describing Antarctica and some cities and their coordinates were described by him. Thus, outlines of Asia, Africa, America and even Australia were drawn on admiral Piri Reis's map. But what about the eastern part of the Earth?

Piri Reis was interested only in geographical points of the strategic importance as he was a commander of navy. Probably, the Turkish admiral analyzed the map once used by Christopher Columbus attentively and then clipped the part describing the eastern part of the Earth of and presented it to the archive located in Istanbul in order to keep the way to *"Spice Islands"*, which were especially important for the Ottoman Empire, secret. What was the reason? According to the history, the Ottoman Empire occupied most territories of the Near East until the beginning of XVI century, so, controlled *"Silk way"* and the way to *"Spice Islands"* and was monopolist in trade of the most expensive silk clothes and spices of European markets. It means that, merchants of Europe had to use other ways in order to go to markets of East Asia. Such ways were described on mentioned map. They were the western way mentioned by ancient scientists and south-eastern way along Africa.

There is no doubt that, Turks had hidden the eastern part of the map as they wanted to keep that way secret and didn't want Europeans to be aware of its existence. But the history of the western part of the map is different, though another part was found in 1929 in Istanbul. There wasn't any need for hiding western part of the map. The huge territory located in the west of the Atlantic Ocean – the fourth continent played a role of "barrier" on the western way to East Asia and Turks knew that European seamen had to overcome a very difficult way in order to reach the eastern coast of Asia. It means that, Europeans had to refuse to use seaway for going to the eastern part of Asia and to prefer land road, which was under Turks' control. So, the admiral Piri Reis had hidden the eastern part of the map in a very inaccessible place.

Another hypothesis can also be mentioned. Probably, mentioned map was divided into two parts before being found by Piri Reis. Columbus had made special efforts for this purpose. It was obvious that, the map was enough big. It might attract people's attention when was carried. So, the sea traveler clipped the part he didn't need of and as territories described on that part were known by people, hided it in one of cities of Italia. Columbus brought another part of the map to Spain after using it for sailing to the New World. Afterwards the map was found by Piri Reis.

I think that, Christopher Columbus had sent the map to Italy, his native town Genoa or to the public library of Florentine by means of the trustiest herald as soon as he returned from the travel. But the map couldn't reach its address of destination. Piri Reis controlled great part of the Mediterranean Sea and often attacked vessels of Spain, Portugal, France, Genoa, Venetia and Vatican during that period. As it was mentioned above, the map was taken by Turks when it was sent from Vatican to Italy in 1505. So, the map couldn't reach its address of destination. I think that, the Turkish admiral had found the map, which was used by Columbus during his first travel, in this way.

A strange paradox occurs. Number of well-known scientists began to decrease in the West after the temple of Muses and Temple of Serapes, where the library of Alexandria was kept, were burned. A lot of remarkable scientists had appeared in the West before that library was annihilated. Probably, there were valuable materials used by almost all scientists in mentioned library. The library had been saved until the age of Macedonian Isgandar. Such hypothesis is convincing enough.

Eratosthenes, who had made great efforts for development of geography, is the author of the valuable work about the Earth.

It shouldn't be forgotten that, the scientist leaded the library of the Temple of Muses. Eratosthenes was a mathematician, philosopher, literary critic, astronomer, geographer and author of epic poems. He had determined the Earth's length with 75 km error.[1]

Piri Reis's map proves that, such maps were known even before the age of Alexandre. Were those maps used

---

[1] Н. А. Ионина, автор-составитель. Сто великих чудес света. Москва, «Вече», 2000. стр. 148.

in travels resulted in significant geographical discoveries?

When I looked through ancient travels, the expedition sent by the Egyptian pharaoh Necho II to the south of Africa through the Red Sea in 597 BC attracted my attention. Travelers didn't dare to start long travels in the ancient time. The expedition had to continue its travel in the Southern Hemisphere after passing the equator. Ancient people thought that everybody, who would try to pass equator, would meet with the hell or fall into the deep cleft. They said that, nobody had sailed in that direction and returned from there. But several seamen agreed to start travel and returned back through the Mediterranean Sea after going round Africa and entered Egypt by passing the Nile River. I think that, they could complete the expedition successfully owing to convenient maps they had. It means that, as Phoenicians had a map similar to Piri Reis's map, they could overcome all travels successfully. It shouldn't be forgotten that, Phoenicians could easily visit Madeira Island, Azores and Canaries located on the Atlantic Ocean.

According to Ch. Hapgood, mentioned map described the world by means of ancient outlines. First of all, continents had been described on different maps and then all maps had been combined on one pergament. Such work could be carried out by Nasiraddin Tusi only. Locations of continents and coordinates had been determined precisely as spherical trigonometry had been used for this purpose. The founder of Maragha observatory knew spherical trigonometry enough well.

Discovery of America by Normans and indifference concerning that discovery

Paolo Toscanelli and Christopher Columbus were aware of Nasiraddin Tusi's scientific achievements. But did they know anything about expeditions of Normans (Vikings) organized towards the north-eastern coasts of America?

Cristopher Columbus had read a lot of books on history and geography when he prepared his project. He wanted to know how long he had to sail towards the west in order to see a huge land area in the west of the Atlantic Ocean. Did anybody tried to sail to the west of the

Atlantic Ocean besides Vogado and van Olmen? The professional navigator had read annals of Scandinavian historians besides works of Marco Polo and other travelers. Surely, he was aware of Vikings' travels towards the north-western part of the Atlantics. But Vikings' expeditions weren't interesting for most travelers. The reason was the map made by the Dane cartographer Claus in 1427. Claus had described Greenland and *"Vinland"* united with the north-western part of Europe on his map.

Thus, land areas were obstacles for seamen in the northern part of the Atlantic Ocean. Besides it, great parts ofthose lands were described in Poles. It means that, it was impossible to sail to those lands.

It should be noted that, Normans had traveled to costs of America 500 years before Columbus. I'll use historical sources in order to lighten this issue.

Over the past 30-40 years, many studies have been conducted on the activities of the Normans. In the 1960s, Norwegian scientist Helge Ingstad discovered in the north of Newfoundland the remains of Viking settlements dating back to the 10th and 11th centuries, thereby announcing to the world that Europeans (meaning Vikings) 500 years before Columbus reached the northeast coast of America and even tried to settle there. Of course, Americans of Italian descent took the news by bayonets. However, the mechanism for further research into this issue has already been launched.

The sensational article was published in the newspaper *"New-York times"* of the USA on October 10, 1965: *"Scientists of the Yale University made a great discovery in the field of cartography – the map of coasts of the New World made by Leif Ericson in XI century was found".*

The map was also published in the newspaper. Experts determined that, the map had been made in 1440 – 50 years before Columbus's first travel.[1]

The Irish annalist of the middle ages Dicuil wrote: "A group of Irish monarchs went to Spain at the end of VIII century and some of them stayed there".

One of Viking leaders Naddod was lost at the result of storm in 867 when he traveled from Norway to Faroe Islands. He approached an island covered with snow by accident and named it Iceland.

---

[1] Гуляев В. И. Доколумбовы плавания в Америку: Мифы и реальность. «Международные отношения», Москва, 1991. стр. 10.

The next Viking to reach Iceland was Swedish Gardar Swavarsson. To make sure the island was in front of him, he took his ship along the coast. The journey took a long time, and during the winter months Gardar and his men had to wait in one of the bays on the north coast. They built several houses there, and since then the place has been called *"Husavik" ("Bay of Houses")*.

Another group of Vikings went round Iceland under the leadership of Gardarin and learned that, it was located on the island. Erik Blonde left Iceland in 981 or 982 and discovered Greenland.

He explored 600 km of the southern coastal strip of the island. Detailed information on this can be found in the saga **"About Erik the Red"**. The Norwegian chronicler Ari Torgilsson Frode describes the event as follows: "...in 985, Erik's large fleet of 25 ships, loaded with cattle and other property, sailed to the new island. In the same year, Bjarney discovered the northeast shores of the New World, 800-1000 km west of Greenland's southern shores. Rumors of the event reach Norway and in 1000 Leif the Lucky with 35 Vikings rushes to the shores of the New World. Detailed information about this can be found in the saga called **"The Story of**

Greenlanders". But it's unclear whether Leif made it to the Labrador Peninsula or Newfoundland.

In 1007 another expedition led by Torfin Karlsfenin goes to the shores of the New World".

Thus, in the lands discovered in the North-West Atlantic, the Normans createresidential settlements and even inform the Pope about it.

Normans established settlements in lands discovered in the north-eastern part of the Atlantic Ocean and informed the Pope about it. As welfares of new colonies were improved, the Pope included Greenland in his eparchy in 1112 and appointed Erik Gnuffson the first bishop of the largest island of the world. Several churches were established in the island. The last bishop of Greenland Alf died in 1377. So, colonial possessions began to decline there.

According to the source of Iceland of 1347, Vikings often visited America 347 years after its discovery.

But there wasn't any information in countries located in the south of Europe about lands located in the west of Greenland. Thus, results of mentioned discoveries were known only in the northern countries.

The historian R. Henning wrote: "Discoveries of Normans made in the western part of the ocean were known in the north of Europe only. Other countries knew nothing about them. Even there weren't exact proofs about existence of countries in the west of Greenland".[1]

That's why Christopher Columbus didn't know anything about Normans' expeditions organized towards the north-west of the Atlantic Ocean. Otherwise, he could take Vikings' routes into account during preparation of his transatlantic project. But it wasn't real to use those routes for Columbus. They were very cold and dangerous for Spaniards.

Achievements of Columbus in fields of geography and history aren't appreciated by the humanity

New ship constructions were made, navigation equipments were improved and new maps of coastlines were made. There was a convenient ground for great geographic discoveries.

---

[1] Хенниг Р. Неведомые земли. Том II. Москва, 1961. стр. 353.

Seamen were interested in ways to India, Chine and Japan, merchants and European monarchs were interested in spices, valuable metals and silk clothes. There were two ways towards mentioned countries: the land way extending towards the east and seaway around Africa. The first way was dangerous for merchants and supporters of expeditions at the end of XV century. That way, which was called as *"Silk way"*, was under the control of the Ottoman Empire. The second way hadn't been discovered completely. Navigation experts of Portugal tried to discover that way and organized preparation of maps, which included outlines of Africa and Arabian Sea.

The Great Venetian map was especially important for seamen and scientists. The eastern way to India had been described on that map clearly. But Paolo Toscanelli had described India in the west of Europe and mentioned that, it was possible to go to Japan, India and Chine by using the western way. The spherical form of the Earth was described on the globe made by the astronomer and traveler of Nurnberg Martin Behaim in 1492. But Christopher Columbus hadn't seen that globe before his first travel.

Even scientists of the ancient time mentioned that the Earth was spherical. But travelers didn't try to apply this idea.

Rudolf Balandin wrote in the book **"100 greatest geographical discoveries"**: *"Columbus had a great role in discovery of the Earth's form, existence of settled lands in Atlantics (Plato's Atlantics) and possibility of going to the east by sailing towards the west. It was mentioned by Eratosthenes and Strabo accepted his ideas.*

Christopher Columbus described the Earth as a pear unlike Ptolemy and Kosma Indopoklov. The traveler called upper part of the pear "Protuberance of Heaven" and had discovered that part during his third travel. It was considered the rank of the Orinoco River".[1]

Christopher Columbus discovered mentioned place (rank of the Orinoco River) during his third travel (1498-1500) and called that place "heaven" of the Earth.

Columbus became very popular in Spain and other countries. His enemies tried to disgrace the traveler.

---

[1] Баландин Р. К. Маркин В. А. Сто великих географических открытий. Москва, «Вече», 2000 стр. 68-69.

Even they accepted Amerigo Vespucci as the discoverer of coasts of the New World.

Valery Gulyayev, who was known as the author of a lot of scientific works, wrote in his book **"Travels to America before Columbus, myths and realities"**: *"Columbus had never been on coasts of North America. He could discover islands of the Caribbean Sea and part of the eastern coastline of Central America (Honduras, Nicaragua, Costa-Rika and Panama) during his fourth travel in 1502. North America was discovered by the English traveler John Cabot.*

Columbus thought that, he had discovered India. So, he is considered one of main figures of the age of great geographic discoveries. The genius Genoese traveler established intensive relations between Old and New Worlds".[1]

If Columbus couldn't organize travels towards the west of the Atlantic Ocean, there wouldn't be any relation between the Eastern and Western Hemispheres. The only mistake of Columbus was declaring discovered lands as the eastern part of Asia.

---

[1] Гуляев В. И. Доколумбовы плавания в Америку: Мифы и реальность. «Международные отношения», Москва, 1991. стр. 10-11.

I want reemphasize relations between Nasiraddin Tusi, Paolo Toscanelli and Christopher Columbus. As it is known, Columbus lived in Portugal and its colonies temporarily and was interested in navigation. His brother Bartolommeo was a cartographer wherever he lived. The most educated merchants learned that profession as it had become popular in the Apennine Peninsula.

Cartography and map trade were considered profitable occupations in European countries then. Bartolommeo Columbus used to buy and sell modern and ancient maps. Probably, he had found copies of maps made during the age of Macedonian Alexandre.

Knowing navigation and coastlines was very important for seamen sailing across the Mediterranean Sea. There was strong competition between Catalan and Italian experts in the field of cartography. Bartolommeo got acquainted with cartographers, geographers, archivists and library directors in several cities of Italy when looked for maps. He got acquainted with Toscanelli in Florentine. As it was mentioned above, the well-known scientist leaded N. Niccolini's library besides carrying out other works. Of course, there were a lot of materials about geography and astronomy.

In general, Toscanelli was known as well-known expert of geography and everybody tried to be his friend. Besides Christopher Columbus, Bartolommeo Columbus also visited the library leaded by Toscanelli when he was in Florentine and analyzed necessary materials kept there. He could be indifferent to strange maps kept in the library as exponents. Bartolommeo was especially interested in the map, which described outlines of the land located in the west of the Atlantic Ocean and wanted to get the map made in Maragha observatory. I think Bartolommeo informed Christopher about mentioned map and he copied it. I have proved that, Columbus had discovered coasts of the New World by means of the map made by the well-known Azerbaijani astronomer and mathematician Nasiraddin Tusi.

Though Columbus could do Spanish monarchs' biddings, he wasn't rewarded by them and the world community as necessary.

But the traveler's services were appreciated afterwards. There is a country, river, state etc. named in favour of Columbus.

The Norwegian archaeologist Kh. Ingstad found settlements, where Normans lived in X-XI centuries, in 60th years in the north of the island of Newfoundland and it proved that, Europeans had traveled to the New World 500 years before Columbus and settled there. So, the president of the USA Lyndon Johnson accepted a law about celebrating the 9th of October as the day of Leif Ericson in 1964. And Leif Ericson began to be known as the discoverer of coasts of the New World.

Of course, the day of Christopher Columbus is also celebrated. But the day of Leif Ericson is celebrated three days before it. Even supporters of Columbus held demonstrations on October 12, 1965 in order to protest it.

I can't accept the decision of Lyndon Johnson. America was discovered by Christopher Columbus on October 12, 1492. But the date of Vikings' discovery is unknown. I think only one day may be celebrated as the day of discovery of America and it should be the 12th of October!

Good offices of Martin Behaim and explanation of questions concerning Brazil

But Portuguese ignored everybody, who had discovered Brazil, especially Pinson and Lepe and noted that the Portuguese seaman Duarte Pacheco Pereira and German scientist Martin Behaim working for Portugal had visited those territories in 1490-1495, but it was kept secret in order to prevent visit of other people. Though arguments were enough, it hadn't been proved yet.

Several scientists note that, German geographer Martin Behaim (1459-1507) sailed South American coasts within one of secret expeditions. This thought is considered frivolous as Behaim was weak scientist and unprofessional navigator. Portuguese exploring coasts of Africa - skilful seamen, captains, boatswains and navigators were masters of the navigation school established by Enrique in Sagrish. In accordance with several sources, Behaim settled in Azores in the middle of 90th years of XV century and it is still unknown what he was occupied with there. In several scientists' mind, German scientist travelled western coasts of the Atlantic

Ocean within secret expeditions of Portuguese and may be approached South and North American coasts.

Historians explain it as following: if Behaim sailed in the Western Atlantic, he could reach coasts of both continents. In accordance with several hypothesizes, he knew territories between Floridian peninsula and Brazil before 1498. Behaim had discovered South America with anonymous captains of Portuguese's vessels and had given necessary information to Cabral for the discovery of Brazil.[1]

If Martin Behaim had reached South American coasts and islands located around it, he had to note those territories on the biggest globe made by him in Nurnberg in 1492. Besides it, he could write special notes about mentioned lands after travels ended. He could also make maps describing outlines of coasts of the New World, which was interesting for seamen as an air and water. Behaim knew that, maps of unknown and newly discovered lands were the most valuable documents of that time.

The scientist's map didn't include any detail about the southern continent located on the other side of the

---

[1] Хенинг Р. Неведомые земли. Пер. с нем. М., 1963, т. IV, гл. 198.

Atlantic.[2] Thus, as there isn't any historical document, it hasn't been proved that, Behaim reached America in 90th years of XV century.

Some scientists note that, even old seamen's maps made in 1440 when the prince Enrique (Henrique) lived, prove that, one of Portuguese's vessels approached today's Pernambuco state of Brazil. Unfortunately, this sensetional fact couldn't be affirmed as there weren't enough documents. The reason is as following: Information about sea expeditions organized in Lisbon was coded at that time as powerful sea countries of Europe – kingdoms as Venetia and Aragon organized expeditions in order to discover unknown territories located on coasts of the Atlantic Ocean and competed with Portugal in this field.

Andrea Bianco had made a map of large territory and had written an illegible legend. In Julia Oldham's (1894) mind, Portuguese had discovered Brazil in 1448. When he read the legend, came to the conclusion that, "one of islands was situated at 1500 miles towards the west". Oldham thought that, it was Brazil, which was situated at 1520 miles towards the west of Green Cape Islands. The

---

[2] Дитмар А. Б. От Птолемея до Колумба. М. 1989, С. 230.

Portuguese scientist Batalia Reich supported Oldham's opinions concerning this problem, but this idea didn't spread through the community.[1]

It is considered frivolous hypothesis as Portuguese sea travelers could misappropriate discovered lands if they reached Brazilian coasts. It was reasonless to keep this fact secret. Portugal didn't afraid of neighbor countries as Castilia was busy with Reconquista, Venetia struggled with Genoa and Arabian pirates in order to be hegemon in the Mediterranean, Ottoman Empire fought with Byzantine, and 100-year war continued between France and England. It means that, Portuguese sea travelers hadn't reached Brazil or coasts near it. But it doesn't mean that, they hadn't organized expeditions in the Atlantic Ocean.

Portuguese discovered all islands near north-western coasts of Africa and Pyrenean peninsula during 45 years and included them on the territory of the Portugal kingdom. Vessels of two Portuguese noblemen, who had sailed to the Cape Bohador in 1419 – Juan Gonsalvich Zarku and Tristan Vash Tashera moved away from the

---

[1] Дж. Бейкер. История географических открытий и исследований. Перевод с англ. под редакцией и с предисловием Магидовича И. П. М., «Издательство иностранной литературы». 1950. стр. 44.

west at the result of the storm, met with the island covered with dense wood and created basis for the discovery of Madeira Island. The expedition sent from Portugal towards the west under the leadership of Gonzalo Velu Cabral according to the task given by the son of the king of Portugal Juan I – Prince Enrique (1394-1460) discovered Azores in 1427-1432. Alvise (Luici) Cadamosto from Venetia and Antonio Usodimare from Genoa discovered Cabo Verde (Green Cape) islands in 1456.

In general, Portuguese sea travelers - Jal Ionsh (1435), Afonso Gonsalves Baldaia (1436), Anthony Gonsalves, Nunu Tristan (1441), Lanzarote Pisania (1444-1445), Dinesh Dias (1445), Alvaro Fernandez (1446), Arish Tinoku (1447), Diego Gomes (1456), Alvise Cadamosto, Antonio Usodimare (1456), Antonio Noli from Genoa (1460), Diego Afonso (1462), Pedro de Sintra (1461-1462), Fernan Gomez (1469), Sueiru da Costa (1470), Juan de Santaren, Pedro de Iskular (1471), Rui Siqueira (1472), Fernando Po (1472), Diego Azanbuj (1481), Diego Can (1482-1484 and 1485-1487) and Bartolommeo Dias (1487-1488) began to discover all western coast of Africa and to prepare for future sea travels.

Thus, Portuguese settled in Madeira in 1425, in Azores in 1432, and occupied Green Cape Islands in 1460. Diego Gomez came to Lisbon from Gambia in 1456 and brought 180-pound gold sand. That gold had been given him by indigenous population in exchange for simple glass decorations. Though this news spread in Castilia in the shortest time, he couldn't carry out his activity in the Atlantic Ocean because of the Reconquista. Portugal used this opportunity and increased influence in the Atlantic Ocean.

Expeditions of Portuguese sea travelers Jal Ionsh, Afonso Gonsalves Baldaia, Anthony Gonsalves, Nunu Tristan, Lanzarote Pisania, Dinesh Dias, Alvaro Fernandez, and Arish Tinoku had explored only north-western coasts of Africa and didn't move away from the coast of the continent before 1448.

There was great need for scientific theories of scientists, navigators, geographers, cartographers, astronomers and mathematicians in the discovery of unknown lands in the ocean. That's why every work of scientists was interesting for sea travelers and organizers of travels. Well-known scientist of Florence lived in XV century and worked in fields of astronomy, medicine, geography and mathematics Paolo dal Pozzo Toscanelli

(1397-1482) had great authority in kingdoms of Apennine peninsula and in whole Europe.

Translation of **"Geography"** written by Greek scientist Claudius Ptolemy lived in II century into Latin made him popular and famous world map made in 1474 brought him fame in Europe. Toscanelli told the king of Portugal Alfonse V that, the earth was round and it was possible to go to India through the west: "I'm sure that, if the earth is round, existence of this way may be affirmed. In spite of it, I send the map I had made in order to simplify your work.

Route in the west, islands, coasts and the place you have to travel have been described on that map. The distance you have to keep from the equator and pole has also been fixed. Though it is known that, the place where spices finish and precious stones are found is east, I described that place in the west. You can reach that place if you go through land..." The scientist, who didn't afraid of wrath of the Catholic Church, defended his ideas in accordance with scientific theories and especially the work by name **"Almagest"** of Ptolemy (he noted in that work that the earth was spherical). Several scientists noted that, it was possible to meet with several continents on the western way to India.

It is necessary to pay special attention to this problem. What did the king Alfonse V think about ideas of the scientist? It is known that, such serious projects and ideas were discussed in **"Mathematical Union"** consisting of scientists, mathematicians, astronomers, cosmographers and geographers and their importance was determined.

The project of Columbus, which was presented to the king of Portugal Juan II after several years, was also discussed in **"Mathematical Union"** and the decision was negative. So he wasn't provided with vessels for organization of an expedition towards the western part of the Atlantic Ocean.

After ten years - in 1484 Christopher Columbus presented another analogous project to the king of Portugal Juan II. The idea of the Genoese seaman thinking that it was possible to travel to India through the west was simple. The earth is round and the largest part of it is land – Europe, Africa and Asia. So the distance between the western coast of Europe and eastern coast of Asia is small: it is possible to reach India, Chine and Japan in the shortest time by passing the Atlantic Ocean through the west. Such thought corresponded to ideas of geographers of that time.

Besides Paolo Toscanelli, Aristotle, Pliny the Elder, Strabo and Plutarch also thought that, such travel might be realized. The idea of Common Ocean was accepted by the church as well. Such theory was affirmed by the Islamic world including well-known Muslim geographers – Masudi, Al-Biruni and Idrisi.

Portugal decided to sign contract with the kingdom of Spain in order to avoid conflict with the powerful neighbor. If the official contract signed with participation of the Pope didn't exist, Spain could impede activity of expeditions of Portugal working in the Atlantic Ocean and pretend to discovered land. They signed contract with Madrid in Alcasovas in 1479. According to that contract, South America came under surveillance of Portuguese and Spaniards kept being hegemon in Canaries. According to the Pope's bull **"Aeterni Regis"**, kings of Spain Ferdinand and Isabella refused all known and unknown lands located in the west of Canaries for Portugal on 21st of June, 1481. It means that, vessels of Spain couldn't go down from the 28th parallel of the northern hemisphere.

It became clear that, Portuguese had given presents to Roman Pontifical Councils. That's why Sixtus IV agreed with all demands of Portuguese.

Besides it, the Portugal kingdom demanded territories of Castilia and didn't deviate from war. But Castilia didn't want to return any span of lands to its neighbor.

The king Alfonso V, who gave up his demands for territories of Castilia could get very convenient privileges for Portugal: Canaries remained as the property of Castilia, but Azores and Madeira Islands were registered as the inseparable territory of Portugal. Spanish vessels hadn't to go below the 28th parallel of the north hemisphere when organized any expedition. Half of the Floridian Peninsula, Anthill Islands, Mexico, Panama and South America became property of Portugal in theory.

The treaty of Alcasovas couldn't last for a long time. Spaniards demanded to divide the world again peacefully after the first travel of Columbus. It had become clear that, there were large territories in the west of lands discovered by Columbus. Spaniard Rodrigo Borgia born in Xativa located near Valencia became the owner of Saint Peter's throne in Vatican. Other interesting fact: the bishop of Aragon was appointed Roman pontificator when Columbus started his first transatlantic travel (August of 1492). He was the second person from Aragon, who was appointed for such high position. First person was bishop of Valencia Alonso de Borgia, who was the Pope with the name Callixtus III.

Now I want to write about unofficial discovery of Brazil again. I consider dates noted by historians groundless. Historians wrote that, Brazil was discovered in 1480 or 1490 (accurate date hasn't been written), names of Jan Cousin, Alonso Huelva, Martin Behaim and others have been linked with the discovery. The most convincing date is considered 1494. Why?

Christopher Columbus completed his first travel to coasts of the New World on March 15, 1493. It means that, Spaniards might reach lands located in the western part of the Atlantic Ocean unexpectedly. But there is incomprehensibility in this question: they mightn't demand territories located below the 28th parallel according to the treaty signed in 1481. Because territories located below 28^0 east latitude belonged to the Portugal throne according to the treaty signed in Alcasovas. In spite of it, Spaniards couldn't sail below the 28th parallel and tried to conceal it.

Every lost day was against Portuguese after coasts of the New World were discovered. Portuguese heard about this discovery first of all after Columbus returned to European coasts as admiral's vessel had approached

Madeira Islands mechanically and had sailed to Lisbon after it. The king Juan II received Columbus in his palace after the discovery was made. The king decided to make decisive steps after that meeting. So Juan II organized secret expedition towards coasts of the New World.

Important maps, which existed in the world before 1507

I came to the following conclusion at the result of recent researches: Columbus had a map of the huge land area, located in the western part of the Atlantic Ocean, even before his first transatlantic travel.

He prepared the project, which he presented to the Spanish monarchs, using that map. Probably, lower part of the southern continent on Martin Waldsemuller's map might be copied from the *"Lost map of Columbus"*. How could German scientists get mentioned important material? Existence of that sensational map was interesting for whole world. I spent a lot of time for investigation of this issue.

I described following facts in my book "**The scientist passed ahead of centuries – Nasiraddin Tusi**" 15 years ago according to the researches of the American professor Charles Hapgood: western part of the map, made by the Turkish admiral Piri Reis (1513) and found at the Topkapi Palace Museum in 1929, was drawn using the map of Columbus.

Before Ferdinand Magellan discovered the strait between the continent and Tierra del Fuego, Diego Solis reached La Plata Gulf and sailed to the Pacific Ocean, Faddey Bellinshauzen and Mikhail Lazarev discovered Antarctica, mentioned lands were described on the map of the Turkish admiral. It is interesting that, there were some similarities in descriptions of the South America by Martin Waldsemuller and Piri Reis. The German scientist made that map 6 years before the Turkish admiral. My suppositions are:

1. Piri Reis acknowledged that, he had copied the western part from the map of Christopher Columbus. It means that, mentioned map existed when Columbus presented his transatlantic poject to the *"Mathematical Union"* of Lisbon (1484). How could Columbus get it? It

is known that, the author of that unknown map wasn't the Genoese admiral.

2. According to some researchers, Columbus learned geography, astronomy, cartography and oceanography owing to Paolo dal Pozzo Toscanelli (1397-1484), who was one the most celebrated scientists of the 16th century, and he applied his knowledge in practice. Most scientists think that, he used the map made by Toscanelli in 1474 when started his travel.

But I think that, it isn't true as Columbus might give up the travel if he considered that, the distance between Europe and Asia was 10000 km to Cipango (Japan) and 12000 km to Chine. It means that, the Genoese seaman get that source differently.

3. After Christopher Columbus became close to the Spanish authority in order share his problems, he showed his secret map to the Florentine accountant. Afterwards Amerigo Vespucci drew everything he remembered on the map. He sent the map he made to Martin Waldsemuller and indirectly made him to name the fourth continent in his honour.

I think Columbus sent the map to Italy, Genoa or the public library of Florence by means of the most reliable herald after returned from the travel. But the map wasn't delivered. Piri Reis controlled great part of the Atlantic Ocean during that period and he attacked vessels of Spain, Portugal, Genoa, Venice and Vatican in order to rob them. So, mentioned map also was taken by Turks on the way to Italy. Thus, it couldn't be delivered to the address.

According to the historical sources, nobody except Columbus and Piri Reis had a map proving existence of the fourth continent (before its discovery). Simply, scientists believed that there were islands of Anthilia, Brazil, Saint Brandan and "Seven Cities" in the western part of the Atlantic Ocean at the end of the 15th century and they tried to describe those islands on the non-standard maps made primitively. Afterwards - within 10-15 years after the first travel of Columbus, any map describing unknown lands located in the west hadn't been spread in Europe except Cantino's map.

Martin Behaim participated in the expeditions organized by Portugals towards the western coasts of Africa for a long time and he had seen copies of some maps covering description of the territories located on the coasts of Africa. However, he didn't know anything about the fourth continent. Nevertheless, some scientists mentioned that, as if Behaim sailed on the coasts between Florida and Brazil before Columbus and made some maps describing coasts, where he sailed.

Historians think that, if Martin Behaim sailed in the western Atlantic, he could reach coasts of both continents. They write that, he knew territories between Florida and Brazil before 1498 by basing on non-convincing grounds. As if Behaim discovered South America together with anonymous captains of vessels of Portugal and sent important materials to Pedro Cabral for discovery of Brazil.[1]

If it is a truth, the cartographer of Nuremberg could describe coasts of the fourth continent on the first globe made in 1492, which was called Erdapfel.

"There wasn't any detail about the southern continent, located on the other side of the Atlantic Ocean, on the globe of the scientist".[1] It should be mentioned that, it couldn't be proved that, Behaim reached America in 90th years of the 15th century as there wasn't any historical document.

---

[1] Хенинг Р. Неведомые земли. Пер. с нем. М., 1963, т. IV, гл. 198.
[1] Дитмар А. Б. От Птолемея до Колумба. М. 1989, С. 230.

Martin Behaim knew that, maps of unknown and newly discovered lands were considered the most expensive documents.

Andrea Bianco had made a map of the large land area basing on unreal ideas. According to Yul Oldham (1894), the Portuguese travelers discovered Brazil before 1448. He had read that, *"there was an island at 1500 miles west"*. Y. Oldham thought that, it was Brazil, which was situated at 1520 miles from Green Cape Islands.

The Portuguese scientist Batalia-Reish also supported Y. Oldham's idea, but that idea couldn't spread in the world.[1] Nevertheless, it can be accepted as a hypothesis as some scientists support it.

The map made by Alberto Cantino in 1502 is considered the first map describing the New World. Existence of the mythical Anthilia in the west of the Old World was often mentioned by the scientists of the Ancient Times and Early Middle Ages. The islands discovered during the first travel of Christopher Columbus were named Cantino Anthill islands. There were writings *"Western Ocean"* and *"Anthilia islands of*

---

[1] Дж. Бейкер. История географических открытий и исследований. Перевод с англ. под редакцией и с предисловием Магидовича И. П. М., «Издательство иностранной литературы». 1950. стр. 44.

the kingdom Castile" corresponddingly on the upper and lower part of the map. The Genoese admiral described Cuba as part of the continent, but Cantino named it an island. How did this thought appear if Columbus wasn't on the coasts of the New World when made that map? The Spanish traveler Sebastián de Ocampo proved in 1508 that, Cuba was an island. What about the land described on the northeast of the map? Was it Yucatán or Florida? Probably, it was Florida. It was discovered in 1513.

Cantino's map – Planisphera is considered decorative art sample. It included route to the New World used by Europeans during the Renaissance. According to the specialists, it was very valuable for that time. The navigation map made by the Portuguese is kept in Italy. Planisphera was made on the pergament and consisted of six parts. They were glued and the whole map's measures were 2 m 17 sm – 1 m 02 sm.

Alberto Cantino was considered one of the most interesting figures of his time. He worked in Portugal as the emissary. Whose emissary was he? The family D'Este was one of the influential families of Italy in the 15-16th centuries. They had a great role in management, collected historical objects, art samples and demonstrated them at the houses as well as Honzagas and Medicis.

Ercole I d'Este, duke of Ferrara was interested in intellectual activities as well as the most rich Italians and got information about expeditions of the Portuguese by means of Alberto Cantino. He was an emissary and secret agent of the duke, who prepared reports on the most expeditions of the Portuguese. Cantino lived in Lisbon and duke asked him information about interesting discoveries made on the coasts of the New World and to send maps of mentioned coastlines to Italy.

It is known that, mentioned map was made by unknown cartographer, but not by Cantino. Cantino wrote to Ercole I d'Este in November of 1502 when he was in Rome that, he bought the map, which could be interesting for the research, for two ducats. The territories discovered during the second travel of Columbus were drawn exactly on the navigation map, which was considered perfect for that time.

The eastern coasts of the South America were descrybed together with mountains on the map of the Italian cartographer Niccolo de Canario. How could the mountains in the east be described there, when Europeans couldn't see mentioned continent? After all, the map was made by Canario in 1502-1504. Probably, the map, which is kept at the National Library of Paris, was seen by Vespucci and the Florentine accountant used it when wrote his letters.

Calculations of the Florentine cosmographer Paolo Toscanelli brought about a fundamental change in Columbus's life

There were experienced captains, cosmographers, navigators, boatswain and seamen in Portugal and seamen became skilful experts in expeditions. But there was a great need for professional seamen in Spain and so, most navigation leaders didn't want to lose skilful travelers as Columbus. And the traveler mentioned that, Spain would use his skill and experience one day.

Columbus corresponded with the Florentine scientist Paolo Toscanelli before traveling to coasts of Guinea. Two letters sent by the scientist to the Genoese seaman were very important for him.

According to most historical sources, Christopher Columbus asked Paolo Toscanelli's advice in 1474. This advice was about the short seaway to India. The Florentine scientist was known as a great expert of cosmography in Italy and Portugal then. He corresponded with most colleagues, who lived in other cities, about his works.

Every innovation made in the middle ages was investigated by progressive minded people. Especially, geographical discoveries were very interesting for people. After the Venetian merchant Marco Polo traveled to Chine, sea travelers of Portugal began to investigate unknown places located in the east of the Atlantic Ocean and some changes of the Earth began to be discovered. Most cartographers began to describe new territories on their maps and presented it to the world community. It was very profitable business. Such experts had relations with sea travelers and geographers. Changes of the Earth's structure were interesting for churchmen too. The canonic of a temple located in Lisbon by name Fernan Martins was a plenipotentiary agent of the king of Portugal Alfonso V in Rome and there he had got acquainted with Paolo Toscanelli. He asked questions about the Earth's measurements and distance between the western coast of Europe and eastern coast of Asia.

Paolo Toscanelli used measurements of Marco Polo rather than measurements of the well-known Greek scientist Claudio Ptolemy when he prepared the project about the Earth's measurement. But other scientists – most geographers and cosmographers used measurements of the well-known Greek scientist. Marco Polo had described coasts of Asia at 30^0 towards the east unlike the Greek scientist.

Measurements determined by Paolo Toscanelli were interesting for the king of Portugal Alfonso V too. Fernan Martins corresponded with the Florentine scientist after he returned to Lisbon in accordance with the king's order. Columbus also corresponded with his fellow countryman. The Florentine cosmographer had sent the copy of the letter written to Fernan Martins to Columbus either. He wrote that, there was a shorter way by passing the Atlantic Ocean in the west besides the way to Spice Islands (Moluccas).

"I know that it is possible to prove existence of this way if the Earth will be considered spherical. I send my map in order to simplify your work. Route of sailing to the west, necessary islands and coasts and point of

destination have been described on that map. Distances from equator and pole have also been written. I have described countries of spices and valuable stones in the west though they are usually described in the east. Those places can be reached in the east by going on the land..."

Columbus was interested in navigation since his early years. He thought a lot before working on important issues. He always desired to participate in great expeditions. Probably Columbus informed Paolo Toscanelli about his project. He wrote to the Genoese sea traveler: *"I congratulate you for your decision to sail to the east from the west. I am glad that, you have understood me"*.

I think that, Christopher Columbus couldn't agree with thoughts of the Florentine cosmographer. First of all, well-known sea traveler couldn't agree with length of the Earth's outline. It means that, Asia isn't situated in the Atlantic Ocean at 10000-12000 km away from Canaries in the west as Paolo Toscanelli thought. Columbus had determined that, land area located in the west of the Atlantic Ocean was at 4500-5000 km away from Europe. It means that, the mentioned land was other land, which was unknown for the Old World.

I think, he agreed with ideas of the Azerbaijani scientist after getting acquainted with Nasiraddin Tusi's *"Zij-i Ilkhani"* and his map and was sure that, the land area located in the west of the Atlantic Ocean was at 5000-5500 km away from Europe. That distance could be overcome in 30-35 days.

Toscanelli was a defender and leader of the public library founded by the humanist Niccolo Niccolini. He defended ideas mentioning that, the Earth is spherical and planned to go to India through the western way. The astronomer had edited *"Table of Alfonso"* (XIII century). Though Paolo Toscanelli had read scientific works of most scientists, he had lessened measurements of the Earth for unknown results.

Experts can't justify Toscanelli for such rude mistake. He had made elementary mistakes when made his map in 1474. But he had opportunities for preventing those mistakes. The Greek scientist Eratosthenes lived in Alexandria. According to his calculations, the length of the Earth's outline was 43625 km and its radius was 6943 km.[1] There is no doubt that, Columbus knew this

[1] R. Qasımov. Konkistadorların Mərkəzi Çili sahillərində faciəli ölümü. Bakı, "Çaşıoğlu", 1999. səh. 247.

fact. As he was interested in astronomy, he had taken into account calculations of Eratosthenes, Poseidon, Al-Khwarizmi, Al-Biruni, Tusi and Toscanelli before starting his travel.

Usually cupolas of temples were used as part of sun watches. The most popular example is the cupola of Santa Maria del Fiore located in Florentine. P. Toscanelli installed his popular gnomon in the temple in 1474 and could determine afternoon moment by means of it with exactness of half a second.

He attached a bronze plate with a hole in the middle of it on the window located on 90 m and made a ruler on the floor in the left of the main church.

Rays of the Sun passed through the hole of the disk and reached the floor in two months – between the end of May and end of June. The device had remained until the end of XIX century and then was destroyed by restorers by mistake.

At the result of inexactness of measurements, Toscanelli lessened measurements of the Earth and determined that, the distance between Spain and India was 6 thou-sand miles – this measurement was two times less than the real measurement.

The French physician Jan Fernell (1497-1558), who was interested in astronomy, wrote that, the length of the Earth's outline was 39816 km and its radius was 6337 km.[1] It means that, Paolo Toscanelli had made a mistake. According to his calculations, the length of the Earth's outline was 29000 km. So, Columbus didn't accept report of the Florentine scientist and took into account measurements determined by the Greek scientist Eratosthenes and geographic coordinates determined by Nasiraddin Tusi.

Of course, my hypothesis is serious enough. As N. Tusi's map was kept in the library of Florentine, *"Zij-i Ilkhani"* also might be kept there. How could Columbus find that work then?

It means that, Columbus got acquainted with Paolo Toscanelli when he was in Portugal. But he knew the Florentine scientist when he was in Italy. They say that, Columbus met Toscanelli in Italy and discussed interesting issues with him… The Genoese traveler was interested in the scientist's works and liked to look through his maps.

---

[1] О. Коротцев. Глобус, как измеряли землю. Ленинград, «Д.Л», 1980. стр. 312.

Toscanelli liked to share his ideas with his friends unlike other scientists. But he kept his sources secret as didn't want other scientists to steel his discoveries. I want to look through a brief historical chronology before analyzing this issue. It concerns Paolo Toscanelli's activity.

Nobody knew how lands and oceans joined eachothers in the Earth. Though Paolo Toscanelli was a scientist, he described Asia for two times larger and ocean between South Europe and Chine narrower. According to his calculations, the distance between Europe and Chine was 2000 liq (12000 km). Cipango (Japan) was situated at about 333 liq (1998-2000) in the east of Chine. Azores, Canaries and Anthelia could be used as stopping places during the passage. Christopher Columbus made his calculations in accordance with books of astronomy and geography. He thought that, it was necessary to travel for 800 liq (4.5-5 thousand km) in the west from Canaries to East Asia in order to go to Cipango. This was a phenomenal idea.

The French geographer of XVIII century Jan Anvil wrote about it: *"This was a mistake and it resulted in great discovery"*.

Did Columbus make the greatest discovery of the world owing to this mistake? Isn't it a miracle? It may mean that: America was discovered in 1492 by the expedition of Christopher Columbus by accident. But this assumption can't be accepted. The discovery of the global importance can't be made by accident.

According to books of history and geography, Christopher Columbus thought until the end of his life that, he had discovered East Asia. It was mentioned in our text-books too. Only pessimist people can believe it. Most people don't believe this assumption.

But they don't investigate facts and only mention that it is an arguable problem. I also can't accept this assumption and so, began to investigate corresponding events. Of course, it is difficult to believe that, the experienced admiral and professional traveler as Christopher Columbus didn't understand that, he had discovered coasts of the New World though he had traveled there for four times. But most experts write that it is a truth.

Columbus got acquainted with the map made by the Florentine scientist Toscanelli in 1474 when he was in Italy. I want to mention that, the distance between Canaries and Bahamas is about 950 liq. According to

Columbus's calculations, the most convenient way to Cipango (Japan) was 800 liq towards East Asia in the west of Canaries. It seems that, Columbus didn't take Toscanelli's map into consideration after he made his own calculations. He didn't need the Florentine scientist's calculations.

There was another unknown map besides Paolo Toscanelli's map. I think, the Genoese admiral made his own map by means of most scientists' calculations and that unknown map and used it during his travel. He had enough information when reached coasts of the New World by means of the Canary current and Passats, so, he couldn't think that, those lands were Asia. As it was mentioned above, he had prepared seriously for the expedition towards Spain and hadn't shared his ideas with anybody besides his brother. He knew that, there weren't unknown eastern coasts of Asia on the other side of the Atlantic Ocean.

Literatura

Абрамсон, М. Л. Кириллова, А. А. Колесницкий Н. Ф. и др.; Под ред. Колесницкого Н. Ф. История средних веков: 2-е изд. испр. и доп. Москва, «Просвещение», 1986.

Авадяева Е. Н., Зданович Л. И. Сто великих мореплавателей. Москва, «Вече», 1999.

Андре М. Подлинное приключение Христофора Колумба. Пер. с фран. М-Л., Земля и фабрика, 1928.

Афанасьев. В. Л. Текст воспроизведен по изданию: Бартоломе де Лас Касас. История Индии. Ленинград, «Наука», 1968.

Бейкер Дж. История географических открытий и исследований. Пер. с англ. М., «Иностранная литература», 1950.

Бейкер Дж. История географических открытий и исследований. Перевод с англ. под редакцией и с предисловием Магидовича И. П. М., «Издательство иностран-ной литературы». 1950.

Бейклесс Дж. Америка глазами первооткрывателей. Пер. с англ. М., «Прогресс», 1969.

Блон Жорж. Атлантический океан.

Верлинден Ч. Христофор Колумб, Эрнан Кортес. Ростов-на-Дону, «Феникс», 1997.

Qasımov R. D. Enigmatic discovery of Brazil. "Lap Lambert Academic Publishing", Riqa. 2018.

Qasımov R. D. Christopher Columbus, Nasiraddin Tusi and real discovery of America. "Lap Lambert Academic Publishing", Riqa. 2019.

Qasımov R. Əsrləri qabaqlamış alim – Nəsirəddin Tusi. Bakı, "Yurd", 2003.

Qasımov R. Xristofor Kolumb, Nəsirəddin Tusi və Amerika qitəsinin həqiqi kəşfi. Bakı, "Çaşıoğlu", 2002.

Голант В. Я. Планету открывали сообща. Москва, «Наука», 1971.

Де Гомара Ф. «Общая история Индий», 1552 г., XIII глава, «Первая открытия Индии».

Горсиласо де ла Вега. Текст воспроизведен по изданию, История государства Инков. Л. «Наука». 1974.

Гуляев В. И. Доколумбовы плавания в Америку: мифы и реальность. Москва, «Международные отношения», 1991.

Гумилевская М. А. Как открывали мир. Москва, «Д.Л.», 1997.

Дитмар А. Б. От Птолемея до Колумба. Москва. 1989.

Дитмар А. Б. Родосская параллель. Жизнь и деятельность Эратосфена. Москва, «Мысль», 1965.

Daniz R. Amerigo Vespucci, Martin Waldsemuller – secret bargain. "Lap Lambert Academic Publishing", Riqa. 2019.

Daniz R. The scientist passed ahead of centuries – Nasiraddin Tusi. Lap Lambert Academic Publishing", Riqa. 2019.

Dəniz R. Braziliyanın müəmmalı kəşfi. Bakı, "Nasir", 2014.

Əmrahov M. Böyük ipək yolu. Bakı, "Mütərcim", 2011.

Ионина Н. А. Автор-составитель. Сто великих чудес света. Москва, «Вече», 2000.

Коротцев О. Как измеряли мир. Глобус. Л., «Д.Л», 1980.

Купер Ф. Дж. Мерседес из Кастилии или путешествие в Катай. Одесса, «Маяк», 1985.

Лас Касас Б. История Индий. Пр. с исп. Л., «Наука», 1968.

Лиелас А. Каравеллы выходят в океан. Пер. с латыш. Рига, «Лиесма», 1969.

Магидович И. П. Христофор Колумб. Москва, «Географгиз», 1956.

Магидович И. П. История открытия и исследования Северной Америки. Москва, «Географгиз», 1962.

Магидович И. П. История открытия и исследования Центральной Южной Америки. Москва, «Географгиз», 1965.

Магидович И. П., Магидович В. И. Очерки по истории географических открытий том II, Москва, «Просвещение», 1983.

Морисон С. Э. Христофор Колумб – мореплаватель. Пер. с англ. Москва, «Иностранная литература», 1958.

Муромов И. А. Сто великих путешественников. Москва, «Вече», 2000.

Письма Амриго Веспуччи. Перевод с латинского и итал. «Издательство иностранной литературы». – В сб. Бригантина – 71. М., «Молодая гвардия», 1971.

Помбу (Роша-Помбу) Ж. Ф. История Бразилии. Пер. с порт. 7-е изд. М., «Издательство иностранной литературы». 1962.

Путешествия Христофора Колумба. Дневники, письма, документы, 4-е издание. М., «Географгиз», 1961.

Самин Д. К. Сто великих научных открытий. Москва, «Вече», 2002.

Самин Д. К. Сто великих ученых. Москва, «Вече», 2002.

Слёзкин Л. Ю. Земля Святого Креста. Открытие и завоевание Бразилии. М., «Наука». 1970.

Страбон. География. Пер. с гречес. Москва, «Наука», 1964.

Свет Я. М. Колумб. Москва, «Молодая гвардия», 1973.

Свет Я. М. Текст воспроизведен по изданию: Путешествия Христофора Колумба. Москва.

Свет Я. М. Севильская западня. (Тяжба о Колумбовом наследстве) Москва, «Молодая гвардия», 1969.

Стингл М. Индейцы без томагавков. Пер. с чешского В. А. Каменской и О. М. Малевича под редакцией Р. В. Кинжалова. Москва. «Прогресс», 1984.

Ханке Х. Люди, корабли, океаны. Москва, «Прогресс» 1984.

Хенинг Р. Неведомые земли. Пер. с нем. М., 1963, т. IV, гл. 198.

Христофор Колумб. Путешествие. Москва, 1952.

Цвейг С. Собрание сочинений в семи томах. Звездные часы человечества. III том. Москва, «Правда», 1963.

Table of contents

Ramiz Daniz

Sensational map found in Istanbul

105 p.

Baku -2022

Translator: Hokume Hebibova
Computer operator: Sinay Gasimova
Computer design: Sevinj Akchurina

Printed in Great Britain
by Amazon

75518107R00061